FABULA RASA

FABULA RASA

a book

BRIAN CHAN

PEEPAL TREE

First published in Great Britain in 1994
Peepal Tree Books
17, Kings Avenue
Leeds LS6 1QS
Yorkshire
England

ISBN 0 948833 59 9

For Molly Ann Carrington

CONTENTS

FICTION

DESERTS

FICTION

FICTION

We can't breathe without it. The fabulist in-
forms the very seed. Even when there seems
no need, the Lie invents the edge of a blade

for us to hold our breath balancing on. If
by certain lies we get to know the truth,
pretending a life we start to leak its blood.

— Such lies shake, wake and mock me up, me to keep
awake, my dreaming sister, to help me
keep realising our birthright and so earn

our sleep, my sleepwalking brother, my memory-
spun virginal twin, my absent-bodied
angel, awake and learn now to keep waking

like a wet-winged sunburst snapping out of its
shell of dreams to shed the hymen of eyes
still too cloudy, not yet fabulous enough.

I WILL DO

anything not to sleep
so that I may leave my doors open
for my enigmas and oracles
to return from the moon with amens
and omens which never ring doorbells.

I like to dream with my eyes open
so that when I do sleep I don't have
to work too hard addressing myself
but can drop in on friends on the moon
where the coffee's fine and the wine speaks.

Yet sometimes a sleeping dream pushes
its head out from under my eyelids
and like it or not I'm left staring
at the hieroglyphic of a text
which my urgent heart cannot deny

but which the sly sun soon erases
or revises into another
version of a fiction of a cloud-
rack of facts that choke and blind, one more
real dream-side of the one sideless dream.

ONE DREAM

There is nothing here
except the knowledge
of a nothing this
doing embodies,
a fiction designed

to disintegrate
(today's meaning is
yesterday's puzzle
and tomorrow's joke):
living forever

is fed by dying
over and over
(a cliché to live
while scorning its name

But there's only one
dream: earth, hell, heaven
are rooms of one house
through which something stalks
us as over-and-

over as we need
rooms to bear, stages
to enact, become
and so know, through its
million fruits, one tree.

ADAM

unfolds
himself out
of the timeless
dream of flesh
and into the seam-
less flesh of his
dream. Not quite awake,
he drifts between dreams
of fleshy flowers and pulsing
rock and knows no difference between
fact of fire and lava of his heart.

Until faithful heart itself betrays
with desire for then and then and
the count, still wordless, begins,
the yes, still nameless, starts
to chart its garden,
to question its tree
and praise its fruit,
to ask its walls
and state its gate

beyond which
everything and
nothing
matters.

ADAM CAELEBS

On a certain morning he awoke,
built a gate to shut behind him, walked
all to the way to a world warmed by work,
dried apples, drugged snakes, cold milk
and pale wine.

There he remains stained by purity,
sometimes recalling a dark jungle
in whose mirage he once tried to build
an oasis fire against
the night's cold.

THE TRIP I WILL MAKE

is the one I am.
The skies will mirror

the clouds of my eyes,
my sinuses will

decide the weather,
mountains will rise up

when I fall, and fade
if I fail, in love.

I build my own boat,
stitch and hammer its

sails and anchor, flood
these rivers of blood

with fish that I eat.
They too are stewards and

masters of all my
deaths and of their own

fate: death's but a shape
of exchange, the price

of forever, one
more gate and bridge: we

know the trip we will
make we've made before

and the trip we do
is already done.

PICTURE A BLIND MAN

crossing a desert, sand of himself,
dragging himself between the edges
of a perpetual plateau of day.

His footprints over those of others,
other authors, other gods become
blind fools, cross: to weave a world of wants

which are like stars issued in daylight,
invisible but soon to be seen
part of the fabric of fact. But his

stars are being crushed under his feet
or scattered too far from any sun
to puncture his eye of endless night.

So he sleeps under a sky whose eye
is as vague or as eclipsed as his
and he wakes to a wafer of noon.

Still it is the sun and moon he feeds
with thought of sun and moon he feeds off.
He is son and father of the sun,

he is mother of mother moon and
of sands rivered and peopled with fire,
of suns charged, of moon changed, by his mind.

CLUTTER

History's furniture: brittle souvenirs
collected by tourists of the desert,
proof of pyramids built on an abyss
reeking with the amnesia of passions
bent straight on their love-affair with themselves,
a tree flowering but bearing no fruit.

Meaning is lightning over the abyss
at night questioning its own existence.

JUSTIFICATION

Over a midnight desert,
a glass-moon always half-empty
leaks its light on to two dogs
ripping each other to shreds
for the right to the shadow
of its drip that proves they are
more than incestuous strays.

PICTURE POSTCARD

Envy my palm-tree/
be glad for my sky
of escape: babble
the best substitute
for response, a genre
a fiction designed
for dashing tourists
of their own bright lives,
the scrawl a pretty
desperate alibi
against any hint
of sadness or change.

COMMUNIQUÉ FROM BRAZIL

The jungle we thought
a maze of free flight
is in deed a net
of tightening knots.

For every vine we feel
we have thrown off, there is
one more imagined real
wrapping round our ankles.

At the slightest slack,
we lunge for light and
air and, dripping, sink,
choke in pools of dark.

The shadows before us
are so dense that we start
to grab straws of glimmer
from grunts of ghosts behind.

But turning, we find
the crumbs of our dead
skins shed to mark one
sure path back to some

idea of home have all
been gobbled by vultures
of our mind's lust to burst
and burn its self-born bonds.

MEDIAEVAL MONKS AND OTHER MODERN MEN

This ghost has not strayed from your hell but is
yet to be born in a time whose best faith
be for doubt, such as you might fain forget,
tied to your fires of world without end. He

has mortgaged all his power to the other
myth that there is no dream cannot end: his

Bomb is absolute, and he feeds it and
himself such fictions as confirm his faith.

Now then imagine his panic when you try
to bind his feet: death for him's an abyss:
into his literalist hell his soul,
if any, has only further to fall.

If you alarm his heart, it may burst out
of his time to spread on to yours a stain
of hell on earth — which finds you anyway
once you insist paradise is elsewhere.

If earth's not also a room of heaven,
you too don't know how to die: you and he
are twins whose mutual haunting now confirms
hell obliges whenever faith needs proof.

THIS MASK

                    of a sleeping
king reminds of who we
are, a people who make
death in our own image
the way we make our gods:
the fiction of memory

is our cathedral version
of the shacks and inns of lives
that remain under the eye-
lids of time like negatives
waiting for the eye behind
time to shine its light through them

to reveal their ghostly essence
of white shadows and grey smudges
that lies smothered beneath the mask
of flesh we wear at a million
winks per second so as to bear
the miracle of light throbbing
at the heart of our hollowness.

NOT A NOVELIST

This blank stare into the face of fire
becomes the slate on which is revealed

the fictional heart of memory
whose scrawls are as grooved as they're fickle

roses in a flash unfolding and
shrivelling or jewelled bugs sliding

over and under the threads of time,
leaving seeds of humour in their wake,

        so ticklishly swift are my vision
        of them and their revision of me,

were I a novelist I'd forget
that humour's vanity unless we

scratch and show the sun itself bursting
with laughter at its noughts-and-crosses

game of ghosts who mock up mirrors of fire
to see what can be made of what is

and who keep missing the glow of black
lava at their own streaming eyes' core.

MOUNTAIN BY NIGHT OR DAY

In fear of the pulsing warmth of this
statement of silence breathing within
us, but without our babble, I think

This is the first naked face, the one
indifferent form and secret before
words mask, clothe, carve, betray and confirm

it figure of our fear of our own
lava nature smothered and clotted
by the rain of its own clouds of breath.

But already more bloody chatter.
However much we try to contain
the mountain, we release it deeper

into its secret flame, it stamps us
wider into red readings of our
masks of dumb black earth or cool green blood.

READING

Somewhere here spirit sprouts
one more mind reading itself
dead leaves of fictional news.

Seeing itself so, can
it ever escape the ghost
of vanity haunting all

its urges to invent
more stages to act on, more
gossip and rows to act out?

It knows it has to choose
the stage that has chosen it:
this act of eternity

the role of Raker is
its exact mask and mirror:
the lines it reads are patterned

on its own palms, walls drawn
and notched with ink burnt from blood,
tears, spit and the dust of leaves.

NEWSPAPER

Yesterday's iceberg and tomorrow's
steel both melt under the scorching eyes
of the insomniac blind reader
of sinking balloons

which burst and spread their poisoned breath in-
to the craters of the desert moon
of his face that begins to crumple
like a map on fire.

JACKRABBIT AT HOLE'S EDGE IN SNOWFIELD

A lost hare's his own home, dreaming
his field to be alone in,
his snow to be cold by, and he
drilled the hole to arrive at.

He knows all this but doesn't want
to know too well lest the thought
freeze his footsteps, melt their path, clog
the abyss with brown grass: then

he would be really far from home
changed to a desert riddled
with mirages of stick and mud,
grey roofs, greyer groves, green graves.

His snow dissolving behind him,
his field looming blurred before,
at the chasm's lip he stretches
down for its voice, his own his

onus: 'You dreamt me here to feel
the fall of freedom, to learn
to spin a spider's bridge across
me, or over and around

me to leap or step — all to un-
dream me as your path across
your snow blurs its footprints' punctures,
knowing they matter only

as working bridges towards this
hardworking anxiety
without which the ever-changing
field would vanish without care;

for if jacks drill holes in the ground
to prove their world is solid,
then they'll have to tend them as you
now plumbing me with your breath

to prove your voice and mine are one,
to fulfil your dream's blueprint
and your path's footprints of sure fear,
fearless doubt and fruitful falls.

I would not be filled with clutter
of clocks, baseless pyramids,
tin stars awarded to racers
who accept tracks aren't also

thoughts, gold not also tin, tin not
also air not also womb
and food of fire. To fill me
with less than fire's to avoid

the challenge you have yourself posed,
the challenge of all dreams: this
of awaking in the dream to
the dream and so extending

it as it exhales its ripe fruit,
inbreathes its new want of buds.
You can close your eyes and step on,
close your eyes and leap over,

can patch my gap with the nearest
plank and plod away towards
one more me, around the corner
or nine lives on. Or you can

erase me with vision cut of
vision, for I want to be
seen for what I am, in order
to become the something else

I like a bud already am.'
And the hole that once drew on
his feet, his groin and his spine now
blurs its edge, folds in on it-

self, fading like a grey whisper,
so that his field is without
a single shadow of any
puncture of black: tragedy

is born of feeling he must choose
between being sucked down one
hole and falling through all others,
while all he can describe out

of existence, knowing it's he
poses all questions of holes,
chooses to plunge and land upon
a new unproofed page of white.

WHAT CAUSES THE FROST

on the windowpane
that prevents
the sun from painting my mind of glass clear
with sharper
ghosts of smoking rooftops and cars and men
of dry ice?
My mind of ice against which my heart breathes
its warm air.

PARVENU'S RAPID EYE MOVEMENT
— a saccade

If every breath I take is not
my dream coming true, the breath I
invoke, then every time I wake
from these dreams to that, I am bound
again to enter the cluttered
but blank room where I keep stumping
my mind against its furniture
of sharp clouds and the drugs of doubt

in the realm whose king's a hanged man
the ghost of whom returns to be
hanged again, even while he's still
hanging, still jerking from the tug
of the frayed but still tightening
threads of a tongue once so golden
with knowing that starred and pointing
fingers of fire burst and flowed

out of it like water, like blood
veining and rivering all dreams
the dream, the clouds and rocks and fish
of the mind, all with the knowledge
of all hearts the one pulsing spark
and seed and food of the sun and
then and then and now the tongue bloats
and scrapes itself on the sidewalks

of the blank city where blind boys
afraid of their own fire keep
fiddling at the foot of either
side of the floating wall of noon,
where bland guards and plotting lords
of the ten-o-clock thesaurus
promise care for cash, keep a dead
freezing eye on our every breath.

AMERICA

A bright shore wakes the drowned dreamer
to his own questions: these are
what he seeks through deserts
of ribbed care or pitched by waves

of desire. To stake some cooling
pool or to be washed ashore
is not to tap the deep
well or discover a new

world but to frame an old still-life.
So the quicksand dream remains
the true rock of water,
the real continent of light.

DESERTS

INVOCATION

Woman of air and rain, flood these deserts
with rivers of breath and pools of cool light;
woman of fire, blow and lick a flame
up the ladder of the spine to the green
centre of love, the blue flute of the Word,
the purple sun at the eye's horizon,
the open crown of the all-seeing queen,
to smooth the path of this blind nightingale
    through the sand dragging its wings
    whose feathers shake with your voice.

TRANSITION

Light's wide relentless knife scrapes
away what's left of the moon
savaged by the dogs of sleep,
splits night's greying egg and spills
an orange stain across these
white shells of yellow shelter,
cuts through the cold lard of sleep,
melting it into the screams
of a million false alarms,
the tears of waking yawns, rank
fat wept by a waxen sun.

BLIND REBIRTH

Cocoons of determined
changes, dreaming a clock's
scream waking them fast from these
bleeding gates, pulsing them down

blind alleys of routine
pain, dumb waves pounding against
deaf walls, a million seeds
flung into a drought of cold

wincing suns, frozen to brick
before the chance of wingsprout.

CONSCIENCE OF A FRUIT KNIFE

This moonlit blade with this window
closing into me pares
these eyes that have cut
one more light, shut out
a child's day, turning a father's night
a dark door on her
eyes: tangled shreds of emotion, moods
by music stamped genres
of response glowing, fading, glowing
like nazi neons,
profound jingles to narrow
vision of the moment
from universe to cell.

A BIG TOWN UPBRINGING

Tenderness, an urgent child, touched
by the midnight rain's sigh, stretches

a dreaming hand out the window
of her heart's echo-chamber and topples

into streets of glass smeared with smashed eggs
of light beside hollow walls shedding cold

shadows that lock their claws into her eyes
and guts and shred her blood to threads

to feed night's spreading cross-stitch tight-
knit by tightlipped spinsters of kissing spite.

HOME

nails your hands
to polished wood, points
a finger in your eyes red
with dreams of bridges which also
prevent your hands and eyes but, so far
unachieved, strengthen their pivot and stretch.

TO A GIRL IN POLAND
— for Joanna Kościuk

It was a small world and yours
was a wide mind. You wanted
the miracle of another
voice hidden in you, one you were
born with, to be recognised.

You wanted a talking thing
whose bell had already called
you to the mystery of the ghost
of words you could fill your head with
and pour your whole heart into.

You wanted to talk to your
self living nine miles away:
it was a wide world to be bridged.
But your father, an army-man,
would keep the world small and far.

Could he remember the power
of a child's desire that will
somehow hurdle its bars of no?

Could he see you setting a clock
to alarm, then hiding it,

so that when one of your selves
came to visit, she would hear
its bell and wonder what it was
and you could announce: O, teraz
mamy nowy telefon!

TO LET

yourself be pulled
by the kite of the 2-in-the-morning moon beyond
your sandy ruts, to let go of
its fine singing twine, to leap from
that taut cloud on to this
firm oasis of windy palms, only
to find the cafe at the end
of the mind, at 2 in the afternoon,
CLOSED
by the dusty elders of decaffeinated sleep,
by the teetotal mothers
of smothering shadowrock.

IN MEMORIAM FRANCIS PAPILLON

The pig that escaped the butcher had
to be caught because men are men and need
no reminders of freedom to survive
their world of blood pressing from left to right.

Thus we spite our heroes of the spirit
by drugging them with our darts of sleep,
locking them in boxes packed with straw
and labelled Witch, Madman, Idiot, Clown

— so that when we do get to murder
them with our vaccines and vitamins and
cameras and chuckling headlines
on the back page of the Sports Section,

we can go to sleep thanking the Lord we
have kept the desert clean this side
of Hitler and never dream of a hell
stacked to high heaven with hogs that are human.

THE SIMPLE LIFE

Querulous cynic, hollow pugilist,
disappointed idealist, bitter drunk,
arrogant ignoramus, pensive dunce,
dumb simpleton, honest questioner,
impish chameleon, bland ape, all these

small-town boys who make up the big town,
who measure and rule their cage of the sky
and plug it with shallow grass and green drugs
and leave it to the wife to choose their apples
and dream of a garden before the fall

BIG CITY FARM GIRL

At the change of her season,
her eyes droop like old windbent
fences with old twisted signs
as snow crowds and shrinks their fields,

clouds and mists her windows
of thick doubled glass, chokes
the trumpet of her throat
to brittle darts of ice,

and settles on the green but
greying lawn of her pursed heart
whose nomad weeds, accustomed
to the return of this cold

evicting touch, simply shrug
with no show of hurt or loss,
drain their tongues of speech, leaving
shrunken brown gestures of care.

A CERTAIN THIEF OF AN UNCERTAIN TIME

Through black maze into green desert
you refine the jungle you scorn
in terror that its voice may be honeyed oil
to your greased syrup, yet you remain
a snake crushing toads while affecting
advocacy of the featherless bird,
laddering your voice to heaven
for crumbs, your hands in your pockets,

cramming your purse which splits and spills
drained bones willing a flood of sand
whose overnight vines are by ambitious boys
axed to crumple and fold like clowning
arrogant adders faster than flutes
can sound, giants crash (flutes refuse to fade),
old vultures return for the crumbs
of a dream of bones, blood and bread.

COURT JESTER,

from narrow noughts of light you spread
your blind father's song, your eyes closed
to dogs hunting rats or rats
gnawing mice choked by traps,

till, no answers posed, your fiddle
seized and shattered, your hands are cut
off, your eyes burnt out and you,
within dark diamonds, shut.

WILDROSE SPROUTS ACORN

This vine, plaiting itself into the trunk
of an oak in the hope of adding
its thorn strength to the tree's empire
(or tree's strength to its own empire)
so surrenders its roses,
its stem's fibre, its seed's
pattern of fire.

TO A COLONIST

You slant by and I know you
as someone who is what he
knows, something so certain it

has no notion of itself,
no name, no voice, only mask
of itself as man with name

and words to say to other
ghosts whose maskness makes you wince
in despair of blind false fools.

You know too much not to be
hiding all hints of yourself
behind your wall of stone facts

by which you try to limit
the world of the mind to your
golden models of a past

a stigma in your eye bright
with anger for a world stained
by your own shadowed vision.

But arrogance is excused
by neither experience nor
ignorance nor innocence.

We either surrender pride
or flag our stones to ragged
fire; either grant stone is smoke

or rage till smoke it proves us
when easy all its walls fall
as hard as we believe them.

VULGAR ROW

— in memoriam N. A. Robinson

Rather than devour each other to two tails
like two whips, stand on opposite sides of a wall
and shout together, listening
not even to yourselves, certainly not
yourselves as played-back music of the lash:
that would serve only to make you
word less. To scream

is all, relief not release of the stomach's stone
that will exhaust you to a righteous sleep of eyes
aching, pressed by rubber-numb arms
crossed backwards in the stretched resignation
of a leaden prayer like the wounded wings
of the albatross of spent sex.
In sleep the stone

will duplicate itself, a snake that wriggles off
in as many directions as chops of the axe,
as flying fragments of your wall
of words made more solid with every blast.

LAST NIGHTBUS

The blown-up moon
is no warmer
than the yellow
streetlamps stooping
like vampire guards.

Scattered seedless pods,
each believing he
is going somewhere,
each wrapped in a fear
that can't feel itself.

A hell of numb nerve-ends,
wounds reknit by the salt
of custom; indifference
without view of response;
concern and love postponed.

All very savage, all very
human: the caves have changed, that's all:
progress the difference between cave
and box, the distances between
traps of the heart strapped to its wheels.

THE SING-ALONGER'S EASE

Knowing the song too well, two bars
ahead of its record-singer
he leaps and drops to the edge
of a chasm echoing his last

squawk like a question repeated
by the person to whom it's posed
who's careful of his answers.
But such caution is another

habit. From the rope of his, hangs
his voice waiting for the other
to catch up, when together
they'll swing across another gap.

LOVER AND LOVER

are now married and so begin
the temptations: to collect things,
people and other sensations,

to pursue pleasure, to expect,
to demand, to grow skins, to look
backwards into mirroring masks,

to measure to sieve, to invent
a future in which others will
serve a fiction of finished love.

ROOFS AND ROADS

As your warm bread of winter sun cools fast
and sinks early, you shut out what's left
of its light to keep the heat of your hands
and heart from any hint of final cold and dark,

turn off the oven, and the green plant-lamps
turn on to start the consolation
of night's sand warmed by your breath in a rough
translation by your automatic gas-furnace.

Your friends are out of town, buying next year.
At their doors you have been love's beggar.
Now you sing in bathroom, dance in kitchen
and leave them to contemplate the fate of their lawns.

When they need their hands held, they will wring them
or smoke them over their mouths and eyes.
Pockets will hide them and wallets console.
Buttons and dials for time and weather and jokes.

If they need help, your hands you might lend them.
Meanwhile you have letters to knock off
to yesterday and books to read you then
and in your garage 2 cars dead but keeping warm.

THE WIND BUILDS

a blockade of snow
up the walls of sleep's eye that wakes
to find its doors cannot open
and its shovels buried outside.

AVOIDING THE WIND

The timeless sun in the breast must be the
source of the cutting wind that returns
on nights like these to scrape the streets
of men who must hide within their cups
or their pipes of dreams, depending
on which side of walls they can afford.

It is the wind of a desert of ice
so inhospitable to humans
that only people can bear it
underneath our stiff armour of clocks
and other promises we make
to ourselves, to avoid our wind-selves,

our wind-knife carving the edge of a dune
of snow as stark and smooth as baked bone,
a beauty so harsh it is best
reduced to a calendar image
beneath which our days are boxed off,
some crossed out, some starred, and all numbered.

PAMPHLET

You've given up on the only case there is
so you must get busy decorating it
with pretty images of desolation
or funny ones of angels and funerals
or with dreams of dynamiting the local
agent of the Hopeless Promise Ltd.,
write letters to your deaf mothers, not meaning
but interest is beauty, what today leaves you
aah is tomorrow's ah-well to be hung next
to the calendar oracle that you need
consult only out the corner of your eye,
so bright are its red exceptions to your black-
and-white mindscape of horoscopes, ads and cross-
words that patch problems and promise hundreds more.

BUT IT DOESN'T HAVE TO BE

this killing, where are the fucking gods,
where are we? I know in order to bear
the sun in our breast we disguise
ourselves as dentists and garbagemen
but why the sloth of hugging these earth-hurts
under our eyelids, eternal
eclipse of our moon and maker? Vain
punks of pain, winking at one another
through our masks, over our fences
against ourselves like the wall we have
around the universe started spotting.

REACTING TO A BOURGEOIS MATERIALIST IN MILAN

What's this about bearable heaviness?
The earth is no mere mud-heap nor is man
a blood-bag that must leak to prove himself
realer than the angels who prevent him
often from spilling. Earth's a stage of love
we enter and exit through swinging doors:
easy come easy go: such lightness is
no stranger to that which we really are,
accustomed as it is to changing skins,
to butterflying between Acts and Plays
through doors in walls always shifting, to being
as Falstaff as now, as Ariel as ever.

TRADITION

— for Bernardo Bertolucci

Dismiss the promise of her open lips
and the black clouds of her eyes:
they intend no word, no rain.
Her great-grandmother's lips are
locked: she will let you unlock
only a shadow from her ashen mask

behind which are hidden sharp-ringed fingers
reckoning your eyes' kisses
like beads on an abacus,
crushing them to a powder
as fuel for the wordless
distortions of another hard glass ball.

TO A FRIEND IN EUROPE

The price we pay for Beauty is all
the warm rules that make you wish you were
back in the desert where everything's

cooler, including the blood, and Talk
To You Later means I Couldn't Care
Less If I Don't, and it's Convenience

that's the conventional smotherer
and the chasms between the boxes
of building and motion and the mind

are bridged by pictures, words and numbers
all as miraculous as they are
ugly (traditionless) or tasteless

(disrespectable) or terrible
(meaningless). But would we be elsewhere
than on the moon of our naked now,

whether strangely at home in Rome or
stranger where we were born at world's edge
on a wall where feather men defy

the wind, or getting lost in London
or New York or finding what we did
not search for in some car-lot or camp

of a town, whether looking over
the shoulder into one more mirror
or shading our eyes from the earth's glare?

The price we pay for vision, for the
mind itself, is all we would prefer
not to surrender: expectations

of how the earth's tilt should rhyme with our
latest fiction of some Future based
on yesterday's cheap Just-so routine.

ANGLO-ANGLE

— for Janice Shinebourne, Frances Shepherd, Marilyn Cox and Sym-Ra Bhatti

At some canting corner of Big Ben's time
is a timeless pub, one of a million,
outside which cars are parked tight one behind
another as cocksure in their skew stalled
stretch as the old bricks of the building's walls
behind which some after-work Londoners
sit solider than stone, lighter than glass,

having first shrunk their cars into narrows
most aliens would not even consider
unless we dare let ourselves be challenged
by the stubborn crotchetiness of things
and learn what the natives know by nerve: how
to skew as many corners as there are
necks to be broken that somehow are not

and especially after a pint or two
when each parked car is jolted from its skew
and zigzagged to another squeeze somewhere
in the same (if the driver's lucky) street
where he lives and oh the towering feeling
to slant a mile in to his pre-supper gin,
the day's final bottle-neck so rewarding.

LION

His house is no longer
bigger than he once its tenant
landlord of a ghost confirming
its spectral rooms temples

of muscle and blood. Now when real sunlight
falls on solid paintings
on wraith walls, they all fall under
the glazed gaze

of a lion shrunk flaccid
in a cage too small
even for a dangling sloth.
Each space between the bars of his cage

is a wall. The sunlight
is stains of bleach streaked across the fur
of a spider-monkey performing at the promise
of peanuts. The pictures are all

of one figure: an orangoutang
clutching the bars in the cage of his heat
and pacing an unchanging chacha of pain
round and round a sterile pole.

MONK MOVING HOUSE

To sing after death and before birth, I am
a bird cleaning and draining its cage of its
furniture of feathered fear, every mirror
and clock I erase. There is nothing I want
to keep but the wafer-and-water regime
of a prisoner of the sun and the moon.
Up stairs I float like dust in sunlight and drift
like smoke through doorways into rooms denuded
of all images. My whole body's a blank
bullet that would not be fired, a bowstring
stretched to a tension without arrow or aim,
a harpstring plucked and silenced at once, a flute
through which the wind warbles its song without time.

A SENTIMENTAL FAREWELL

— for Sandy Nicholls and Jim Meers

You are the town of which I am too strong
a stranger: I'll never know your cool light
enough, though I've charted its stars of dust
that virus my veins too close to my heart
for it not to dodge yours still free of this
autumn ache of shedding the sun's blood, this
spring rain of dripping salt leaves of warm ice.

I will but cannot return: to what bones
of summer, what ghostly fictions of fall?
But I will be some day one more town you'll
enter as stranger and embrace as ghost
only to pass right through towards the next
memory, so matching the guilt I feel now
freezing about my heart as I leave you

shrinking and disappearing like a star
below horizons in rearview mirrors,
a dot that's the seed of the map of love
sprouting myths of staying, or moving, on
so that remember means the same as miss,
if remains the only answer to when
and history another name for loss.

NOTIONS OF A NATION

— for Rod Trentham and Charles Meggison

A space other than the room we
are sitting in, talking about the
Other we will never be but are.

An apple with a definite
shape and flavour but nine-tenths rotten
to the mites on the other tenth's rim.

A Problem somehow to be solved
by our Achieving a Consensus
then turning back to our unsolved lives.

A disease to be invented
so that we can have something to be
diagnosed if not die from or for.

A club we are dying to join
for which we must produce credentials
impossible by our own standards.

An ideal state we can never
achieve so that our disappointment
can flatter our sense of our own worth.

A Future we cannot afford
not to invest in, lest our children
curse us for leaving them less than Heaven.

A Promise whose spirit of Real
Estate keeps trickling out our fingers
to wrap itself round our hands and feet.

A tribe we must worry about
before it's Too Late and it breaks up
and we're left wandering in a desert.

A land stolen from other tribes
we give some back to so they'll have no
excuse for not cleaning up their act.

The world's widest campground where all
tribes may pitch tent and mock up the dream
of Kafka's Amerikan Circus.

Strands of rock and river and road
woven slack by the keepers of light
that confounds the terms of earnest men.

BALLAD OF THE SAD SALAD

Today I indulged in the crime
of digging up dandelion weeds:
in order to serve the rabid I-
deal of a lawn whose green is uniform;
in order to show my neighbours that I
am not beyond being obsessive like them;
in order to prove to myself I take some
interest in the way things around here are going;
and breaking my neck to root out my love for you
that is fast taking over my entire being.

But dandelions don't take no
for an answer, no matter how much
we make them scream and bleed with our knives,
chemicals and other splendid weapons.
They're a stubborn bunch of squatters and have
a million relatives waiting in the wind
to descend like refugees who don't fit in
and yet haven't got a hint of self-consciousness
and are not in the least bit apologetic
about turning up and grabbing a piece of the pie.

I understand dandelions
may be used to make salads and wines.
Wouldn't it be a better idea
to *cultivatve* the buggers and let them
have the illusion of freedom within
a closely guarded arena so that we
get to control and use them at the same time?
Our fertilisers would make sure they grow fat and
weak and turn into something less threatening, less
doggedly shifting, something I daresay more *human*?

GHOSTWATCH

— in memoriam Malcolm Lowry

The bus entered the town and stopped
at its station. I checked my wrist,
I don't know why, since I was in
no hurry. Always the last to step
outside to grab a piss, a bite,
a smoke, I saw from my window
a man, an Indian, with a twitch-
ing face. I guessed he lived in town
because he stood in the doorway
of the station restaurant, his
hand on the doorknob (like he owned
the joint), and looked into the face
of each traveller going inside,
looking for, hungry for, something,
and each time he looked with the start
of a one-sided smile that did
not get beyond the cracked wrinkles
at the side of his eye into
his eye because all those passing
through the town, looking for something
else, passed straight through him as though he
was the waiting open doorway.

When I was ready to stretch my
legs, I moved towards him and saw
his face had settled for again
its twitch rooted in a thousand
unfinished smiles, his eyes were pinched
and squinting into a distance
not my eyes and his hands had moved
into his pockets. For something

to do, I checked my wrist (we were
doing good time) and bought a Coke
and hid my face behind some smoke.

A BEGGAR DROPS IN

When his face shows up at your door,
you sigh, for you know it is you
you must meet while he visits
himself, talking moon as though money
were mere and he master of his
moons. Ghost gazing into a glass,
he plucks your eye off your rug and
polishes it bright with his breath
so that you cannot help seeing
what you know he contains of you.

At the first hint of your latest
yawn, he sighs like a dog resigned
to hunger and pretends to leave,
and your relief is mixed with fear
of the you you'll always now need.

NATIVE STRANGER

When you step off the 'plane, you are another
but clinging to an idea of yesterday
and knowing which pocket holds your papers help
to prolong the useful fiction of a you.

Other familiar shapes of pictures and words
are waiting to pick you up and lead you across
the gaps between the impressions of a man
you must keep flashing so as to keep breathing.

The no-nonsense look in your eyes reveals you
to be a betrayed lover bent on revenge-
ful reconciliation with a city
that's still switching on and off as much as you.

When you stride through its tight streets you are floating
on the air of the knowledge that you don't have
to live here but in your stomach is a stone,
a mushroom tough to vomit that you'll have to.

Old loves and aunts are here to prop your fictions
and you've brought them the appropriate presents
to celebrate what you now call their courage
to have stayed in a place you still can't quite stand.

You keep opening drawers that smell of anguish
you recognise though it no longer fits you.
Yet you keep coming back as though to witness
that running from spectres makes them more solid.

But the surer you think them the stranger you
feel, for what you see most clear you're farthest from.
Near the hotel door closed your suitcase you keep.
Next to your heart your passport like a shield sweats.

A REUNION

We are the ghosts of greedy lovers settling
for sloppy kisses between the closest
mongoloids, hollow reeds gurgling in the mud
of memory's guts, wordless flabs flogging,
flagging another flood of conviction.

REPETITION

You come, you look, you repeat, knowledge and
        experience
a game of articulation. How to explore without
cataloguing, without all these callous-forming,
        skin-grafting
words, without ghosts lending a misleading hand over
        breakfast.

Shadowed by past moons, the day can only yawn: will the
        sun
derail the slow night-train destined once more for the
        showers of gas?

AN EASY ROAD HOME

Two cars ahead of mine, two more
cells in a tree's bloodstream, started
branching into opposite veins.

Cars are made to keep us as lonely
as we make them: I'd kept my
distance and didn't have to brake

but like a hot knife cutting through
butter that spreads and trickles off
to left and right, I split their path

and each drained to a house like mine,
a nest within some crotch of nests:
it was all very regular.

But what do the gods make of mites
crawling up and down their thumbnails
only so as to stay apart?

Size has nothing to do with it,
of course: each cell assumes itself
all — until this or that knife proves

this is so by threatening it. Then
call the ambulance and police:
set them wheels a-rollin' tribal.

THE WINTER MEN

We ride a forking
snake of ice whose wheeled ruts prove
us the sheep we think
we're not as each chases his
crumbs of siren gold
sprinkled by the yellow ghost

that drives us. So the snake di-
vides us while claiming
to connect, leads us, between
our smoking temples
of warming yawns and dumb sleep,
through stray clouds of flat
freedoms and the mirages

of space and speed, and into
the numbing smooth scars
of redundant distances
sentinelled by trees waiting
in naked silence
for the snake to fade,
for men to melt, and spring to speak.

REALISATION

one morning sculpted by frost, moving
uphill home in a warm quiet car

with no speaker prattling and nothing
behind me but a whole world draining

like a child's milk and the spreading clouds
of my most uncluttered dream rising

before me like the cool but warming
breast of a disinterested wet nurse

RETURNING TO AN EMPTY HOUSE

Putting the key in the doorlock, I realise
on the other side there is nothing but a me
that's bound to be everything or else is nothing.

You will be gone for eight hours and so will I.
Eight hours are a wink or an eternity,
a house with man of spirit, or mere ghost, inside.

I close the door behind me and am everywhere
beside, within you in another house, wall-less
mansion of the mind with nothing but love within,

no duty, no expectation and no desire
to restrict the path of the heart into one rut
whose walls must close in on love like time on the eyes.

THE ROAD

is still throbbing in me after
my wheels have stopped.
They have brought me to this point I
cannot escape
even when I chase promises
of paradise
and am chased by threats that the clock
will stop and stay
set one way like a sun with no
light left for day.

My body, still buzzing with speed,
is an elec-
tric knife making aimless slices
in this morning's
sapling space that begins to seep
yesterday's and
tomorrow's dreamblood every time
I close my eyes
to remember where I am and
where I must be.

Last night, having bridged the chasm
of false distance
between fictions of there and here,
having agreed
without question that this is where
our minds are now,
you and I like sharpened blades clashed
and cut through each
other without shedding a drop
of blood or love.

Then into each other we rained,
washing away
every scrap of dead skin piled up
along the road
that separates strangers asleep
in the same bed
of dream-roads that cross each other
on their way in
to the one town of love where all
roads meet and melt.

LANDSCAPE OF LOVE FROM A SPEEDING BOAT

The brown blur of trees on this side of the shore
is the dense desert of words we decide
to hug so as to keep the green mist carved
on the other side, on the other side.

FOR JANE SIBERRY

But tenderness is hard
to inhabit. Skins and masks
to be shed. Every act is
a pretence of yesterday's.
The pain of love, what more, what?
These stirrings of raincloud.

FOR SYM-RA BHATTI

Whirlpool of your voice, blurs
of your face: a love all
smoke without flame, flood with-
out rain, calm without storm,
  bloom without branch, tree of air
  whose root veined and split our heart.

I MISS YOU

I sketch you a cloud determined
by the conceit of my wings dripping
your vapour into a desert pool
of gentle derision I failed

to drown my pride in like a cat
that surrenders its crackling belly-
fur to the mesmerising glory
of a sunbeam's cosmos speckled

with planets of dust drifting in
and out of being at one with the
light's revealing whisper. I missed you,
so this remorse for a mist long

drifted or rained out of being
whose smoky memory now mocks these clipped
hands scrambling erasable scratches,
a cat's paws clawing at the light.

EXCHANGE

Then the breadth of your bright planes
shamed my pinched well of shadows:
why dig for black gold
when I could kiss a battery of the sun?

Now your face's thin golden
shadow stabs my wide white night
revealing you sucked
down the silver maelstrom of your dark faith.

MUSE,

to be chosen by you
is bread I cannot buy,
the bread of breeze and rain
in a desert of sweat,
of dry tongues. You're the wind
that carves the shapeless sand
to hills and pools for moon-
light to define and fill.

APPOINTMENT

Having resigned my calling
as your angel, I saw mine
pass in a red sky and waved
with greedy arms just in time
to break your
latest fall.

ANGEL,

if I could find the words
to replace you, you
would fade, a statue of cloud
that promises rain, then melts
wordless.

But in silence we still speak face
to face and within
each other, recognising
speechless rivers of light no-
where mapped.

God the frustration of words and
of no words, these hands
itch to pluck the fruit that must
fade in the touch, the taste and
the name.

I almost broke our talking wings
by stroking your breast
full of the milk of the moon,
but the moon of no desire,
no word.

Again, angel, fall and shine in-
to this square of dreams
where sun and sea meet as storm
becoming cloud becoming
no rain.

FOR IRINA CHERNYSH

How does one out of many
reply to many in one?
Can mirror answer mirror?
A bright abyss between them.

IN A CROWDED BUS,

                                        and in the staggered cry
of a winter sun falling like a leaf, one
translucent winebottle of an angel floats
before me, her wings wrapped around a cello.
Her stare's mask tries to hide, and so reveals,
her naked flame in a nude balance only
love can disturb. Just as I want to   hear her
voice herself her instrument, a hollow
that needs her touch to feel and so know itself;
just as I surprise myself by wanting her
voice at its purest moan of total control
over itself and of total surrender
to that which needs to be heard — when with one hand
she'll point and plot a path to the peak and flood
of her blood and milk, moons and rains, wine and tears,
and with the other bow and pluck the flaccid
vibrancy between her knees into a taut

fire — just then she throws me

a chameleon's tongue, a spider's sticky twine
of a frown so ancient that it drifts like dust
in the sun's sighs and I am staring into
the heart of a fearful silence the other

side of music or of any other
spell that knows itself and so can speak for all
spellbinders with a love indifferent enough
never to say no even when it is
saying never and none, I am staring down
into the dry well of loneliness where lies
a mummy wrapped in stale air against the ice
whose flag now seems the very sun denying
it absolute reign, so that I feel compelled
to reach out for my own cello's neck to fret
a cry for all the other silence's sons
whose songs of light might be muffled by their own
muses turning a cold eye and ear on them.

RECOGNITION

Though it is a sadness, knowing
that knowing must be enough, if you see
deep in the dungeon of a stranger's eyes
a flicker reaching out to confirm yours
— two masks of mirror facing, paring and
embracing each other's nude enigmas —
know that such vision flames only beyond
the sticky entanglements of the web
of flesh and of the dream of time which lock
recognition down the need that enslaves,
blinds and addicts, and gasps for more

GHOSTDANCE: TEMPLE TO TEMPLE,

we lead each other, feathers
rainbowed by moon light,
through a forest of screams and whispers,
the whole world throbs in your breast

like a bird's, our fingertips
feed each other's spine
a desperate saline, our temples flash
signals of smoke from charred words,

we whirl into the centre
of a ritual fire
that unmasks desire as nothing
but two kindling wings of wax.

PILGRIMAGE

to your tower of promise and desire,
dodging chasms between fading stairs up
to this naked glass cracking roofs of sleep

TO A WIFE

Your obsession with your duty makes
you customs officer
to my love: I have nothing

to declare of it to you even
though the most secret pouch
of my heart is full of this

golden drug that you once discovered
and seized for no reason
but that it made you feel full

of power. But love overbears itself,
can't stand the weight of its
own fruits of repetition

and sleep. Yet I hope mine can still move
you before you become
one more warden of the jail

where love locks itself, itself to think
free, a captive serving
life, an artist of escape.

LIGHT YEARS

We sat in a darkening room
and didn't speak, as though we were waiting,
without knowing we were waiting, for some
thing to happen, as though we were

elements of a design try-
ing to figure itself out, to resketch
an idea of balance that was erased
before it could complete itself.

We smoked and pretended to be
charmed by Brahms; you kept glancing at yourself
in a picture I made before we met
of a woman waiting for her

self in the eyes of another
to unlock her from her self-possession;
but your look was scrutinous and showed no
empathy for her yearning eyes

I now dared not look into lest
I should respond to their pain as to yours,
on this side of the dream where dreamers' eyes
are often dryer than their pain,

or as to my own as I reach
for a world in you too strong for passion
that still keeps waiting to be wanted, freed
by another world's seeing fire.

WE TALKED

                    in a room full
of the child's light I read
in your eyes brimmed with the pain

of need. The room grew dark
and love. Behind you night
crept through silent blossoms fresh

with raindrops that again
will fall when the wind shakes
the petals from which they hang.

CLOUDWALK

The wind and sun collaborate
in a kindly balance, the grass
nods and points towards a new church

still being built whose steeple draws
me on along a ridge towards
you. This is one way of being

within you as you drift away.
So the wind dandelions know.
I think of picking two for you

but decide against offering you
bleeding things and leave them to breathe
without fear. Near the church I see

I can't yet get past the façade
of an old beauty taking new
shape too early now to enter.

But now's the right time, late enough
to turn and hurry back to you,
making flowers wince as I run

to meet you dripping green rain
through cracks of the new spire pointing
in the clear distance that we share.

LOVESONG

Whenever it's raining at midnight
I'll be taking a walk and towards you.
It's your coat I'll be wearing when I must go back home.

Everywhere young men are paid to slam
bullets into one another's bodies
but this can't stop two souls from containing each other.

People are still dying in hunger
but somehow I keep enjoying these grapes
and bergamot tea with you at 2 in the morning.

From now on 2 a.m. is the time
I'll be knocking on the door of your dreams
to make you burn the butter for the next day's omelette.

Before the clouds dry up, let us go
walking in a different town of our own.
Wherever we stop to eat, we'll insist on plum wine.

Dream this town whenever we must meet
as mutual angels full of voice and tears.
Wherever we walk, the moon will keep her eye on us.

I kiss the back of your neck before
it fades with you down your road without me.
The shifting cloud mirroring your steps is your best friend.

AN ONLY POSSIBLE LOVE'S

a pattern of light erased

as it is realised,
filed behind the eyelids

of time a sharp negative
never to be printed, words

in exile from idea,
a wordless life sentence.

THE SENTENCE

confirmed.   by strange tongue.   in ink.
words walls of stone and steel.
no argument.   one choice.
life sentence or death.

But while serving it, there is
no question of not
putting yourself in the hands
of the thing always about
to be born again: the magic of breath
that keeps inspired the slave in his cage
of whip and work, and the prisoner in his
of debt, surrender and love.

In either, words fall, rocks,
or break into flight, birds,
or confirm the silent prayer
of the clock's hands at midnight

or noon.

THE BOOK

PLAINER AND PLAINER

my confusion
of voice and eye, nothing
left to prove or
improve: a plain peace

sculpting certain
ghosts drifting in and out
of time, the wind caught
by an ancient curtain:

sketches of essences,
graphs of a stare
whose centre is any,
whose aim is all.

THE BOOK

fed the boy, the idea
of the book, the idea of the book
of ideas, the smell of the blood
of it, the taste of the meat
of them: boxes and walls

of words for a boy with his mind
set on the freedom of surrender
to words, keys to their own prison,
the worlds they dream and shape to
describe, describe to change.

A boyhood later, nothing has
changed, the book recedes like a seashore
in a rearview mirror, it seems
a parent outgrown, a door
not worth reopening

on to a passageway well worn
and into a too familiar room:
a bored old boy begins burning,
one of the boys, books like bread:
beer's a better idea.

— In the moonsand of nothing else
a dry man stumps his eye on the rock,
the green ghost, of a book left open
like a crossword puzzle un-
finished with clues ignored.

Heartless he tests, hungry he tastes
wonders of noonshadow and moonlight,
of sand and cloud, of rock and rain:
river inventory, first and
latest book of himself.

ON BEING INVITED TO WRITE A NATURALISTIC MUSICAL

We have to write books in order to have
something to read ourselves awake.
For most, the world is book enough, open
enough, sleep enough, dream enough.
But for us walking in a direction
different from that of the world's
and wind's path — this temptation to retell
Don Quixote or Robin Hood
in celebration of that urge in us
that is dismissed by mature men.
But I'm afraid to choke what we would breathe,
either by knitting our heroes
with pretty sheep's wool from the spinsters' pile
or by shaping a brilliant new
mask through which we stare through the spinsters' masks
of All's well with our sleepy world.

In the meantime I simply do not care
whether Robin wore sheepskin tights,
green hose or pantyhose. By such demands
of verysillylimitude,
Hamlet should have been written in Danish
and no one, as every one knows,
speaks or thinks in anything but bad prose.
That Marian did or did not
exist is a pettiness for spinsters
pinned to the tyranny of Fact
that hovers between them and the real world
of their reading revising minds.
The Maid lives because we have mocked her up
like the very bodies we wear.
She has always been because she now is
a breathing shifting artifice.

So when you say 'the story is all there',
I'm sure I don't know what you mean,
for, whether green or rotten, neither tales
nor words will behave or stay put,
and it's not a job of which words to use
but of letting language write us,
of knowing which stains of ink to erase
so as to let the bird emerge
from the frozen walls of its cloudy cage,
to let the windmills turn without
the wind, to let the wind again become
the arrows whose angle it shapes
towards the aim of the mind they pass through,
to start, and keep, breaking the lines
of the tyrannical army of words
that shoots poisoned gas at our eyes.

But look around and see how many line-
breakers now have hits on Broadway.
To sing a song of sixpence has always
been easier than to read a psalm:
I know this from my own experience in
both the bathroom and cathedrals.
But since I'd like to keep our lunatics
sacred, and not turn our heroes
mere madmen, I leave the Don and the Hood
and all their vulgar company
to the vulgar company of my mind
as night falls and we keep walking
up the wind that now and then knocks over
soldiers or Bishops of my own
cursing and whistling in the dark for the
other wind, for an other song.

THE WIND'S ART

Pen, paintbrush, piano, pan
are smoking scraps of his mind
and time back into the wind
that through his bones blows as he
an old horn always the first.

There's nowhere to go from here
but where he is, where the wind
keeps blowing for the first time.

He keeps no broken ladder
to the heap of skins we call
stars, no ladder runged with stars.

There is only the peeling
of hardened skins, the melting
of fat too fat to feel fat,
the slow drilling to the core
of the heart where the wind's flute
floats.

THE IRON POT

needs no stirring, needs no me
to interfere with its
stew no one knows who started.

The sauce, though genius to certain
men, is simmering for all.
I add my own milk and honey,

thanks to cow and bee, grass and bud,
sun and rain. The fire that steams
flows through our nostrils and our veins.

Waiting to taste is a bridge
to the moon and hunger
sprouts more fruits of fire and flesh.

THIS NUDE

of living stone, lava delayed in time,
utters the scars of its sculptor who thinks
what he has shaped is a figure of the world's
pain and love of pain and worship of blood.

But is there either world or pain except
a man and his faith in a world outside
the orbit of his own dreaming blood, a world
he wants to shape with his nude's flame, coming

always too close not to set both ablaze?
In terror of his own fire, the one fear,
he locks away his nude or he smashes it,
no matter: his nude has altered our blood.

The sculptor minds, thinks he has kept or lost
something but his nude's only another
cloud of brick shelved or scattered just as he is
only one more dream of an avid ghost.

Other dreams read of the nude what they will:
how much can they ignore blood, recall ghosts?
Dreams locked in a focus of blood can only
breathe like frozen stone longing for new fire.

LANGUAGE

the spark that leaps
from the base of the spine
and through the guts and heart to
the tongue ignites
into a flame of words that delights
at first in its own shape
and then begins to question
the power of the space it has
fictioned and defined by flashing
into being and so withdraws
down the twine of its own tension
to reseed itself
an ember of silence waiting
for the breeze of another breath.

A WEEK OF NO UKRAINIAN

— for Elizabeth Forster

To become again a child
without words, listening
to the music of meaning,
reading a smile's silence.

To be children and feeders
of the sun of language,
taking from, and making of,
its light a flame of love.

With bridges of light, to shrink
deserts into seeds, con-
nect all shores and make wider
and deeper the one sea.

BLIZZARD VISION

On to a white page of the mind
and against its dark walls
these words of wind blow and pile up.
We are among the dunes
of night complete with desert light,
a beauty that can be
glimpsed only out of a corner
of the eye that the wind
makes sure blinks not to be blinded.

POETRY

                    is too what keeps me from it:
my noisy neighbour I can't begin
to hate, the public liars I love to,
the gate that won't keep shut, the butter
I can't afford, the toe that gets stumped
when I'm happy, the stairs I trip on
to jump awake to screams that keep me
awake and dreaming and
                                        from my dreams.

CYCLE

Letting desire go
rolling like a ball of twine,
I find myself in the green
silence of a timeless sand
I've never left,
and where desire is the seed

that keeps sprouting these
dandelion weeds of time sculpting
and masking the nameless wind
that erases them back to dust.

TO A DAUGHTER

He never hoped for you, he never not:
it was you who gave birth to a father.

A baby, you wanted often to play
with the only friend you had all day long

but the drug of Work would pull him away
to a desk, piano, easel or stove.

If he felt you were keeping him from other
life like salt running out, he might bark

Leave me alone, in the anger of fear,
and he would feel his voice quiver your spine.

But you never stopped running to embrace
him, teaching how gratuitous is love.

Your father's love for you, shadowed by pain,
clouded by duty, was never as free.

Yet though you're now 'tall as a lantern-post',
you still sit on his knee and hug his neck;

but that he once frightened you still frightens him
should he snap Leave me alone, meaning now Don't.

A DREAM OF WOMEN

In a library that smells of French polish
and the suffocating perfume and
powder of its ruthless guardians

floating and sliding in silence between
rooms and stairs and corridors of these
bowels in which a manchild stores

his awe of calves and knees and thighs staring
back at him from below dress-hems raised
smug behind the low issue-desk,

books he has chosen like whores the ladies
dress, undress and press a future on
with fingers whose nails and rings wink

with a promise denied by lips pursed down
and by eyes, like those of humourless
tigers, set within thick stern black

and though he offers in return for their
stony stares his bricks of smiles and thanks,
he can feel them not feeling him

and hurries his whores home to bed where they
engage and release him into dreams
of unmasked pain, terror and love.

FR. MC CLUSKEY'S WORD

So you've had a week of much
interesting guilt, pissing on your
mayor's lawn, screwing turtles,
shooting up with paraffin,
getting drunk on your own blood.

But you who want me to hear
you hurting so towards heaven
will sooner or later sink
under my well-drilled earwax
unless you can strain your facts

through a mask that clarifies
your gossipy vomit into
the clear candle of a voice
so that I might hear what you
know, not what you've overheard.

Without such masks, confession
is a sin, of dear indulgence,
a vat of syrup that needs
draining to be filled again
with acid, mead, honey, rain.

THE OLD

stiff lady with the weak heart, stretching
for a piece of frozen meat just beyond
the grasp of her fingers, I didn't help,
afraid I might insult her independence.

But had her heart snapped there and then and her frame
to be removed to another freezer,
my guilt would not have let my own heart not
burst like a sorry flood of sympathy cards.

'I never saw her again': the hardboiled mask
over pain's face; and yet this same mask keeps
feeling most itself. Poetry is too
the front of a real and essential garden.

Whether I polish the grain and trim the grass,
whether I leave the wood rough and the earth
sprouting intractable herbs, I keep on
seeing her again and again

WORK

As I prune these verses inside, outside
a boy is turning the soil to make it
easier for seed and sun to translate
the one's silent secret into the other's
bright bursting utterance of seamless tongues.

As I clean up these verses, my daughter
is vacuuming the rugs of our dead skins,
sweeping the kitchen floor of our spilt goods
and you are shining mirrors of your own
bright eyes with sweet vinegar of your sweat.

All this doing I once resisted now
I embrace as love's natural mask without
which love would collapse under its own weight
of a vibrant space waiting to be filled
and stretched by a million masks of the sun.

Listening for my own voice, I hear also
the music of other tongues worlds away
leaping up through the stalks of my green song.
Plumbing my darkest heart, I shape the glass
of plain mind in which you may taste your own.

ECHO

Sometimes, while playing a weary piano
or whistling to myself like a caged bird,
I hear something of a mocking echo
like a sharp shadow's softer second edge
that both questions and confirms its first.

Listening more closely for this other voice,
I skip a beat or lose my theme or else
my entire desire to scratch on the air
those noises with which a man furnishes
cells of silence, loneliness or despair.

A new silence spreads, in which the flutter
of the double-edged note becomes a bird's
voice against the vanity of loud plumes
and this ghost voice now buzzes with my blood
tired of pretending it's not the sun's song.

CLEAR CLEAN NET

When there's nothing left
to be said, there's this
music to make one more and
less oneself: into it
I drain myself, drain
myself; into me it pours
its power: I am
a hollow
fish floating in its
swelling river.

REAL SLOW JAZZ

Voices taking time to make
time feel

both tauter
and stretchier than we would

know from the limping clock,
the pace of the heart sure

beyond the need to run across
bridges of love, statements

of the tension between spark
and flame, spirit and flesh,

the tears of gods only men,
of men brimming with light.

THE MASKED MAN TO THE MADAME

To the tango of blood that hurries,
woman of green, waltz only. Across
the cobra's forehead that burns as it
tries to climb your ladder of fire, drape
your snow veil. Wait until night to drop
your buds and thorns on to roofs of sleep
and to the moon's flag a feather kiss.

SONNY STITT'S SAX

A voice like a boy's sure scrawl
of question marks across a blackboard
of silence, a chalky scrape
whose tails fade to fine points as though they
are their own firm erasers.

HOMAGE TO MISTER BERRYMAN

One by one the leeches drop off
my desert plant of questions and blanks
whose cool sap chokes them like a mirror
that will answer neither yes nor no.

Leeches drain one another, eat
of themselves: it is their business and
they know no other, it is their stage
and they must have their play of blood

while my cactus, though it does stretch
its arms, seems to fold them: not a trace
of its milk leaking from its nipples
of needle and its fruit a mere

half-moon of meaning awaiting
the werewolf who, fed up of leeches,
pregnant with hunger for his mistress,
will round out its light with his need.

THE VERBLESS TIME

INSOMNIAC

If your night does not include
questions of the moon before
the sun denies all questions,
the so-what seed set at your core begins
to sprout you a fever that chokes
the very centre it defends.

THE MAN WHO SELDOM SLEEPS BUT IS

always preparing his bed will
leap between moons ignored in our
time but fathered and fed by suns
to ours bridged by the glue of light,
the link of love. In his spare time
he laughs more than he is seen to
and smiles less, as he wonders when
his next moon, and how his last bed.

BUSINESS AS USUAL

In night's grave beyond my floor
one more motor throbs like Poe's
heart, a gaping door's
slammed shut
and another ghost moves on
to his latest rock of smoke.

I who know no rest must feel
such stabs of proof that other
hearts will refuse to stay put
as edged mirrors of my own
pursuit of nothing but breath

so that when some other knife
of night splits my heart enough
to make this dream of blood burst,
I will have been well rehearsed
in both leaving and never.

LYRIC
— (with Joanna Rychert, *after* Galczyński)

Death? you're most welcome but

I'd give anything once
more to saunter through town
at last without a care,
humming Brahms' first Ballade

under windows where fire-
flies buzz their own shocking
songs with perfect timing
and heart, lit from within

like floating rooms of light
which the noonday shadow
in men slowly invades
with ranks of solid ghosts.

What if it's impossible
in my zigzag way to
give life some shape
as other, straight-line men do?

What if the world's only
as green as girls baking
cakes and crows using fresh
sprigs to build old old nests?

THE VERBLESS TIME

when you can't sleep and you won't
hammer nails into midnight walls
to hang more pictures of black-and-
white starvation for real hunger

and you no longer feel compelled
by the clear voice of your uncalled-for horn
to link with its echoes of light
the walls and roofs of a city silenced

by all its dark whispers and dreams im-
pulsed to the shapes of screaming absence
lurking, like starved dogs in black streets,
in corners of rooms ghosted with men

AT THE EDGE

                    of sleep my eye drains itself
of a tear perhaps only the dregs
of my latest yawn. Yet, straddling the chasm
between that dream in which the heart is
a heel sinking into its own blood's sludge
and these others whose wings churn the air's
clouds into showers of stars, I cannot fool

myself this drop is not the sun's oil smeared
by a moonless sky's dry tongue that, slaked,
would whistle and dance with the carelessness
of a flame-drawn moth a buzzing stitch
over the coarse cloth of the nearest fair-
ground cluttered with crippled clowns, joking
killers and forgers of predictable books.

WEREWOLF'S BABBLE OF HIS MISTRESS

At first a bright burst yolk, she spreads up
from behind our shells of sleep and on their rims
balances a bubble already

a ballooning kite starting to tug
back towards heaven the rivers of our veins,
reminding us we're gods of the flesh

— spark of the seed, ocean of the womb,
lava of the heart, sun and cloud in the eye
of the breather. In an open field

two gods enjoy their new wings like windmill blades spun
by the breeze of her smoky watery light.

THE BEFORE MOON

The shadow of our world falls
across your face of light also
our own. Life is insufferable and

I bear it the way a flower
does its plant, a man his father,
man the sun, or the way I will have

to bear your total eclipse
whose dark blood will stain the one night
we use to learn again not to curse

the blood-blooming sun every
blasted day we bleeding wait for
to whitewash our blinking nights. Do I

complain? Not to you, lady:
I know you will return to fire
these bald rivers with your sucking tugs,

know they will soon again leap
to the light of your face full how-
ever scarred by your own
grey craters.

INTERRUPTION LONGER THAN INTENDED

Fifteen hours later, fifteen minutes
seem a naif's dream. I of course myself
disturbed since no one but I magnets my
experience and now nothing's neglected

or unattended, only un-
finished and only as an i-
deal of a then that neverthe-
less exists because imagined
and left demandingly undone.

THE OLD TEACHER

Once words of light flooded the prison, leapt
the wall, of his youth, defying time itself
and blind men saw in them their most painful
ghosts rise up at last out of the dungeons
accustomed of their silence, dying men
heard through a bored boy's pinched voice their
most sacred guardians' secretest hymns.

Now racked raging between the shrinking walls
of age, this stunted boy cannot hear a hint
either from the saints in his cellar or
from his bright angels as they float about
their own routine of family and friends
and his tongues screech like chalk scrawling
noughts and crosses across his mind's black board.

EMILY'S NECTAR, PABLO'S GUITAR, MILES' ALL

At the bottom of the sea,
a stone screams. At the stone's heart,
silence spawns the blue word,
the blue note, the blue blue.

FEAR

reaches for a word
to whisper or scream
at its beloved.

Fear reaches out
for flesh; wastes it-
self growing skins.

Its voice bores
the sure ear:
the whore's sore.

*

Dying alone, no friend,
doctor or priest to prop
the fiction that you have

lived, you reach to clutch at any
final voice and see at the end

of the arm of a stranger with no
number or word in mind the strangest
hand of desire minding its own

business of clinging to one more
straw of its habitual mind.

*

This cup full of hot milk
is a clock hearing
its glaze crack. Break.

The milk needs to escape
the cup that's dying
to be drained. Drain.

Milk must flow and cups shrink
back to waiting coolth:
empty. Empty.

*

Not to waste breath
in an eternity of fear
but to stare through

that which frightens
(a night street of mad dogs)
the mask in the mirror

(that which frightens),
down into the knowing
heart (which frightens) always

sparking itself out
of the stops it makes in order
to keep starting.

THE BEGINNING OF TIME

Even as the earth draws
it back down, the bird
shot in mid-
air flut-
ters forward to savour
the last breath
of a lifetime
of next ones.

DESIRE

            fuels itself
burning itself to ash
whose embers wait for the wind

THE RAW SNAIL

at the edge of her stage
of awareness heavy boots step over.
She would feel their throb
were her world not all throbs and her edges
all numb: it won't matter if she falls
off, she will continue to crawl
like cream down a slope that knows
no base, no backward glance.

The snail's reality
is sparked by the same spirit
as mine and knows her stage as her
peak, though I may see it valley or
plateau: mischief to interfere, pity
a cage of kindness.
With a single touch like a seed to sprout
her memory nine lives hence, leave her raw.

A SUMMER MOSQUITO

Trapped overnight in a cage
big enough for humans but for him
too small, he struggles
to penetrate dawn's glass door
the way, from the other side,
the sun has no trouble doing.

If I slide the door open,
he'll cling to the very walls he would
escape for that is
all his current consciousness;
that transparent barrier is
his wings' field of faith and fire.

He is and is not the sun
he clings to, his father and
mother and son. He is its
flame blinded by his own light,
prevented by his own shape
of light trapped in its own cage.

Seeing him so and not i-
dentifying with his will tempers
mine to help free him. Clinging
to light, light himself,
he escapes himself, fading
wave of light through sand of glass.

DISCONTENT

Master of a deserted castle,
he is sated with lack,
the spices of his food are boiled bland,
his dawns promise green sand.

He longs for a golden Sahara
where at night lions loom
and melt and the sand is smoky and
warm like a pool of breath

and every breath is a grave sprouting
palms so green no night can
darken them and their dates shine and fall
like stars for hungry ghosts.

While sane men and worried wives alarm
themselves with the pointless
hunt of the rat of fear and custom,
duty and sleep, his heart's

drawbridge trickles like sand underneath
the knees of fat beggars
as he waits for its moat to be bridged
with webs by the spiders

of light in whose convent is his true
home, of seeds sprouting stars,
of the one wanton egg flaming new
suns in the nest of night.

HEATER AND FREEZER

feeding side by side
from one electric
breast, yet one making
of that milk a fire
and the other, ice

— one to hurry my
blood and bones and flesh
through cold corridors
of time and action
that never sate this

distancing impulse
of muscle and nerve;
the other to stall
the blood of dead prey
from bursting out its

cells of active death
back into the field
of the flame that be
before lightning bit
into a dry tree,

before the idea
of ice invaded
the vein like a dark
shadow at our cave's
mouth: a hungry beast.

A CHILD'S PICTURE BOOK OF PAIN

Again: a chicken gorging
a cockroach with legs that scream.
Chicken, without legs, floating,
all neck and beak and eyeballs.

A few spasms of muscle
and the work is done: part
of a meal, of a world
the end, of course. Not

that the cockroach minds: it knows
this is how it must resist
shedding the skin it must shed: death's
not a word it scares itself with.

Again: a flash of crocodile
all jaw and teeth and eyeballs,
dragging a child of eyes that scream
down to its underwater vault.

The ballooned corpse will be shared
with a thousand other teeth and
the crocodile may defend but
he won't mind, he also eats fish

and chickens and chefs (CROC KILLS COOK).
But how many words of teeth already
has the child to learn to forget? How
many teeth of words have the child.

HALF A HERD IN A WHOLE FIELD

Sprawled out, except for one still
                                        standing,
frozen hot shadows generating the sun
of their blood, ghosts dreaming the light
they need to magick plain green
to cream of red, gold of white,

or these gifts waiting to share

or to the whispers of their
sea and rivers listening

or in silence hurrahing
the speech of their being
an eternity without
   the name that cages and blinds,
   the word that butchers.

THIS INNOCENT TREE

                              is the tangled tongue
of the beast that feeds off the screams it breeds:
the fruit that falls when the tiger leaps,
the blood of a man that slakes these roots.

PICNIC

The sun melts angels into water
as dogs of sand slash screaming trees,
till light reminds the slept
volcano of my eye the sun
can burst in a man a desert or parch
his tongue beyond denial of rain.

I wake, a cloud shadowed with voices
I must release, a mouth spitting
lightning and bled of smoke
by light addressing itself
in a shifting mirror of water
knitting the very sand it erodes.

BELOW, HERE, THEN

An adder of fire that stifles lies
on the bedrock of the well it has drained,
welcomes the bucket all hands and no eyes.

A desert slave smiles again to feel the
promise of his sweat's reward: heart of cloud
seeded by a sun whose only other

pity is the night.

THE BLIND

man's eyes of sand glint
with the fire of diamonds indifferent
to those who watch, the whole world
to those who can see, a map
of the mind's city complete
with blind alleys one-ways and exits

His gait is that of a ghost crossing
a tightrope as broad as it's
long: he can afford in this
life only the one fall that always
falls in the middle
of things sharp and bright and clear at last.

EVERY NIGHT

this nun's prayers drain
her hollow totem of its fire,
so hardening its tyranny
over her days that, even after
dawn casts its promise across the white
biscuit of her breast, it crumbles
throughout the day like a vampire
in a coffin of sunlight.

HAVING TO LISTEN, HAVING TO REPLY

Here it seems is an end to all effort: this
chasm cannot be bridged, fenced as it is
by its totems of fate: accept this corner-
chair reserved for nodders, as her voice keeps
smiling its furry tears: 'It's my fault again.'

—Yes, lady, everything's everyone's *fault*.
But does everyone wear a halo of pain
as proof? The silent stranger behind us
clamping her fingers of fear over our eyes
and into our spines dripping acceptance
like salt would vanish if we would only turn
and embrace her as the moment's sister
who only comes to shed the shadow that proves
the sun streaming through these windows, these eyes.

RED FOX,

lead the mourning woman of twilight ice and smoke
into the heart of your forest of summer snow
and prove to her neither midnight nor noon's a joke:

uncover for her the split in the rock of night,
show her it bleeding moss of coal as it waits
for the rise of earth's blades through the descent of the
        sun's.

SEASONS

In the fields of fire, no room
for doubt.
        But beneath the sighs
of August, roots still warm pause
in their stretch to dream of walls
of ice within which there is
time for all questions leading
to the last.
        Beyond the glass
of thaw, a crackling river
rises like a bath of light.

WINTER'S FIRST WINDOW

The heart wants to name itself
something else, finding itself afloat
in this womb of pause,
this aquarium of air full
of feathered fish fat like the first

feel of infant fingertips
and, without help of the wind, still fast
falling to confirm
a depth of silence that is
the music of the heart before

the wind returns to lay siege
to our citadels of sleep with its
bass horns and ladders
that make the heart start counting
its beats and measuring its graves,

before the racket of glass-
bubble men, whose winter is black ice
across blank paper
or the crack of stick and bone
within a ritual arena,

can scrawl once more across this
clean slate of rich emptying, this wide
whisper of the heart,
the frenzied maze of our high-
ways of time again, again time.

A ROAD IN WINTER

The sky, however grey, is still the light
that mothered us and to which we must all
return to fill with other dreams like this
that, grey, moves nevertheless uphill and beyond.

INDEX of first lines